Advance Praise

Mandar Kulkarni has created a deceptively simple masterpiece. *From Team Player to Team Leader* is packed with bite-sized kernels of time-tested wisdom. Keep this book on your most accessible book-shelf and reference it often and you will become the kind of corporate team leader that corporate executives favor and great corporate players love and admire.

Coach Dave Buck, CEO, CoachVille
CoachVille is the largest online coaching training institute and a Social Network for Coaches

This is a very useful tool for any new team leader. The book points out key fundamental ideas for being an effective team leader. It clearly highlights the key areas to concentrate on. The book is very easy to read and follow. In my 25 years of management experience, I wish, I had a book like this which I could have handed to many of the team leaders in my group. They would have been successful lot sooner.

Prakash Deshpande,
Senior Director, Oracle Corp.

FROM TEAM PLAYER TO TEAM LEADER

Success Mantras for New Managers

Mandar Kulkarni, MBA, PMP

Outskirts Press, Inc.
Denver, Colorado

From Team Player to Team Leader
Success Mantras for New Managers
All Rights Reserved.
Copyright © 2008 Mandar Kulkarni, MBA, PMP
V3.0

Outskirts Press, Inc.
http://www.outskirtspress.com

ISBN: 978-1-4327-1784-1

Outskirts Press and the "OP" logo are trademarks belonging to Outskirts Press, Inc.

PRINTED IN THE UNITED STATES OF AMERICA

This book is dedicated to my parents
Vasudha Kulkarni
and
late Prof. D. K. Kulkarni

Acknowledgements

The idea of this book was first suggested by my personal coach Diane Seagull. Thank you Diane for sowing the seed.

Once I started working on this book, my mom has been continuously asking me about the progress. Without her push, this book would not have completed.

Two of my friends, Sujata Joshi in Pune (India) and Jashoda Bothra in Vancouver (Canada) helped me in editing the manuscript and gave me useful suggestions. A senior friend and my previous manager, Sanjeev Ukhalkar took time to carefully read the manuscript and suggest valuable changes. I wish to thank them all. All remaining errors and mistakes are mine.

Thanks to Dave Buck and Prakash Deshpande, who were very kind to read the book and send me their feedback promptly.

Some 28 years back, my close friend Jyotsna Athawale had presented me a beautiful pen and asked me to keep my writing art alive. While publishing my first book, I want to thank her for believing in my writing abilities.

Table of Contents

Introduction

The first lesson of being a leader: learn to
    say no. 1
Recognize the initial 'suspicion' towards
    you. 2
Delegate everything that someone else
    can do..3
Effective delegation is a new skill to learn. 4
Use learning opportunities from
    delegation. 5
Delegation is a form of one-on-one
    training. 6
Your role is changed and not you.......................7
Your people are your power. 8
Your first and the foremost goal is to build
    trust..9
Show that you care for your team. 10
Forget "treat everyone equally";
    embrace "individual uniqueness".............. 11
Learn to communicate using many ways. 12
Develop focus... 13
Give yourself permission to make
    mistakes.. 14
Don't be intolerant of failure. 15
Learn to listen. 16
Practice active listening...................................... 17

Tune yourself to the frequencies of an
    individual.. 18
Listen to what is being said. And also to
    what is not. 19
Attune yourself to listen to the "awkward
    silence"... 20
Listening is showing that you care.................... 21
Calm that chatter in your head........................ 22
Practice single-tasking while listening............. 23
Listen to your own reactions............................. 24
Smart leaders ask questions, don't
    suppress them. 25
Questioning is an important tool....................... 26
Think before asking.. 27
Questioning is empowering. 28
Ask questions, do not interrogate..................... 29
Do not just ask questions, understand
    them too. 30
What you do not ask can haunt you. 31
Acknowledging: The skill with the highest
    ROI.. 32
Don't wait to acknowledge. 33
Acknowledge by offering more authority
    and responsibility. 34
Acknowledgement could be done
    without spending.. 35
Create your own acknowledgement
    fund... 36
Leader is also an advisor................................... 37
Share your personal experiences. 38
Challenge your team. 39
Don't get trapped into something you
    can't sustain. 40
Give constructive feedback. 41

Over communicate. It never hurts. 42
Be aware of your new role while
    interacting with your manager. 43
Learn how to interact with the higher
    management... 44
Your peer managers are your resources......... 45
Don't miss the opportunity to develop
    yourself. 46
Make your meetings meaningful...................... 47
Continuous improvement is a key idea........... 48
Don't hide the bad news. 49
Team building needs your efforts. 50
Accept that politics is natural in any
    workplace.. 51

About the author
Contact Us

Introduction

It happened accidentally that I became a team leader for the first time in my life. I was given a responsibility to manage a team of 15 people without any prior notice. We were on the site at a client company and without even thinking what is right and what is not, I started leading a team. I must thank those team members from my first team, who not only accepted me as their leader but gave me their fullest cooperation without any reservations. Perhaps that is the only reason I survived that first assignment as a team leader and continued leading teams for last few years.

Last year when I started to learn personal coaching principles, a light bulb flashed in my mind. Had I known some of the personal coaching skills when I became a team leader for the first time, perhaps I would have done a much better job as a leader.

This feeling prompted me to explore more on the topic of how to apply personal coaching skills for the new managers. This book is a result of that exploration.

I did not want to write something lengthy and heavy to read. Instead, I wanted to create very practical, ready-to-use tips for a new manager to use in his day-to-day life. Perhaps something a new manager can read quickly the night before he starts playing a role of leader. The current format was born out of this need. I sincerely hope that this book serves the purpose and helps a new manager in his new career as a dependable, reliable resource.

I would love to hear from you what you like in this book and also what you don't. Please share your comments and thoughts with me at *Mandar@MillenniumMantra.com*

Mandar Kulkarni

The first lesson of being a leader: learn to say no.

Perhaps you are surprised to see this tip at the top of my mantras for a new leader. It is not a trivial matter and you should take it pretty seriously. Until now, perhaps you have accepted every small and big task that your manager has thrown on you. Your plate has always been full and over-flowing all the time. As a team player, you thought that this quality makes you a good player.

Enter the leadership game. With your changed role, there will be many more things thrown at you. Not only by your manager but also by other managers, your team members and perhaps by your manager's manager, the big boss. You need to be very mindful of your role and responsibility as a leader of a team. Learn to accept only what you can realistically deliver and skillfully reject everything else. It allows you to focus on doing what is truly "your responsibility".

Recognize the initial 'suspicion' towards you.

When you become a new leader, you are entering into a completely new role. It makes people suspicious about how you will perform in this role. It is perfectly normal.

Don't be disheartened. It takes a lot of effort, patience and time to establish you as a trusted leader. Just be true to yourself and do what is right.

Delegate *everything that someone else can do.*

Learning to delegate is one of the struggles of every new leader. Until now, you have done everything yourself. No more. As a leader, you will have to handle a lot of complex situations, juggle many priorities and take bigger risks. Only when you delegate those mundane, routine tasks to others, you can free up yourself for these new challenges. It is utmost important that you learn how to delegate effectively to become a good leader.

Effective delegation is a new skill to learn.

Delegation does not mean that you ask someone else to do your work and forget about it. There is much more to learn so that delegation is effective:

- Select right person for delegation who is responsible.
- Define how to measure success upfront.
- Establish in advance, the consequences for unacceptable performance.
- Create a reporting system so that you do not loose touch with the delegated task.

The above techniques are easy to learn and practice, make sure that you learn them quickly.

Use learning opportunities from delegation.

When you delegate, clearly define the quality of the results, time spent and level of authority granted. After the delegated task is complete, compare the results with your initial expectations and make adjustments.

You can learn a lot about yourself and also about your team members' abilities to perform. The learning derived from delegation is valuable.

Delegation is a form of one-on-one train-ing.

When you delegate a task, understand that you are offering one-on-one training to the team member who is working on the task.

Make yourself fully available when a delegatee needs your support in clarifying the idea, sharing failures or just to be in touch. You are sharing your knowledge, expertise and experience with him in this process. This is an important way of training your people. Don't adopt an attitude of "Delegate-it-and-forget-it". Neither it is fair to the delegatee, nor to the task that is being delegated.

Your role is changed and not you.

When you become a team leader from a team player, what changes is your role. The core "you" does remain the same. Many new leaders start behaving differently when they assume new role. This will confuse the people around you and instead of offering their cooperation, they will start withdrawing.

In your new role as a leader, recognize what you are and be yourself. Your team will be much more comfortable with you. You will have to learn many new ideas and skills to become a good leader. As long as you add these skills to what you already have to offer, you are on the right track.

Your people are your power.

This reads like a cliché and you may wonder why this tip even needs a mention. It is still included just to reinforce the powerful truth that some new leaders tend to forget. You will be successful only when your team is successful. A leader cannot deliver the results without his team. Just focus on how you can contribute to your team's success, your success will be ensured automatically.

Your first and the foremost goal is to build trust.

What is the topmost goal of any new leader? What should he focus on when he assumes his new role? The answer: build a relationship of trust with your team members.

Why? Every successful new leader solely depends on the team members for their expertise, experience and performance. The team members will share these assets freely only if they have trust in their leader. It is up to a leader to step up and make efforts to build this trust. He has to extend his hand first before he expects anything from the team.

Building trust takes conscious efforts and time. You have to build it by your actions, not by words. Effective delegation, mentorship and coaching, fairness in rewards and recognition, and consistently "walking the talk" will help you build the trust over time.

Show that you care for your team.

People do not care how much you know until they know how much you care.

In your role of a leader, you are like a head of a family. For that you don't have to be a gray-haired, serious-looking "grandpa". If you can demonstrate that you care for your team members, they will reciprocate in more than one way. Showing care can be through your actions and also through your words.

Forget *"treat everyone equally"; embrace "individual uniqueness".*

The conventional wisdom says that the team leader should treat everyone on the team equally.

In practical life, you need to understand that each of your team members is a unique bundle of strengths, choices, style, blind spots and hot buttons. As a great leader, you need to learn how to work well with each individual that makes your team. When you are successful with an individual, then you will be successful with your team.

Learn to communicate using many ways.

As a team member, perhaps you have never bothered to think of communication beyond writing an email or leaving a voice-mail on someone's answering machine. As a leader, you will be required to communicate with a different set of people using multiple other ways. If you have not already done, learn how to write a report, a formal memo, how to organize material using slides, how to present in front of a group and how to interact professionally with the higher management beyond your immediate manager. Assess your communication skills and work diligently on adding new tools and techniques.

Develop focus.

However efficient you are, you can't do everything that you want to do. Instead, focus on what makes biggest impact and deliver it.

Learn a difference between what is important and what is urgent. All urgent things are not necessarily important. You need to focus on important things to be truly efficient and effective.

Give yourself permission to make mistakes.

As a leader, you must not be afraid of making mistakes. Allow yourself to make mistakes. It is the only way to learn and grow.

Make sure you learn from them and don't repeat the same mistake again.

Don't be intolerant of failure.

Although clichéd, the idea that failure is a step towards success could not be stressed more. As a leader, when you allow your team members to fail, it creates an environment where people can take risks and experiment. People thrive and develop when their mistakes are accepted and allowed to improve upon. At the same time, it is important to ensure that the same mistakes are not repeated. Forgiving people when they make same mistakes more than once is a sign of a weak leader.

Learn to listen.

We all "think" we listen well but most of the times we just "hear". Hearing is an auditory function of a human being, listening is a skill to develop.

To understand the difference between hearing and listening here is a simple formula: Hearing + understanding = listening.

Practice active listening.

Active listening includes much more than simple listening that is defined in the previous tip.

Active listening includes verbal responses, paraphrasing and appropriate body language. It is a skill to be mastered by practice. The more you understand why active listening is important, the more you will start practicing it.

Tune *yourself to the frequencies of an individual.*

As described earlier, every team member has his unique needs. So as a leader, to understand specific needs of a person, you need to be attuned to him. It does not happen easily. Initially you may not tune into someone perfectly but conscious efforts will certainly increase your ability to tune yourself to your team member at his own frequencies.

Listen *to what is being said. And also to what is not.*

The basic purpose of listening is to understand what a person is saying. More importantly, the leader also needs to listen to what is *not* being said. Develop skills to observe and make a mental note of the volume, tone and pace of the speaker. Observe the body language of the speaker that goes along with his words and you will also listen to what is not being said.

Attune yourself to listen to the "awkward silence".

When you notice that someone on your team is reluctant to open up, you can be sure that something is boiling in his mind. This happens when the team members do not feel safe or do not trust the manager.

As a leader, you need to understand this behavior and take extra efforts to offer your support to get the team member open up.

Listening is showing that you care.

In today's fast-paced life, it becomes very rare to have someone who pays attention to you, let alone listening to your story.

Through listening, the leader demonstrates his/her interest in people, his/her curiosity about them. A leader with good listening skill stands out from the crowd, giving his team members a feeling that someone cares for them.

Calm that chatter in your head.

At any time, a leader is surrounded by so many things that there is a continuous chatter going on in his/her head and mind. Clear this chatter before entering into any formal, work-related conversation. It helps you focus on the conversation itself and engage in it fully.

Practice single-tasking while listening.

Quite contrary to the glorified multi-tasking capabilities, the new leader needs to learn how to single-task while he is in a meeting with a team member.

Ignoring emails, instant messages, phone calls or pager beeps is a better practice to follow. It sends a positive message to the speaking person that he is important and what he is saying has a value.

L isten to your own reactions.

A leader needs to notice and understand his own reactions while he is in the discussion with a team member. It is likely that other team members might have similar reactions for this person. This becomes especially important when a leader is listening to a complaint or a conflict. By monitoring your own reactions, you can better gauge the reactions from the outside world and handle the situation more efficiently.

Smart leaders ask questions, don't suppress them.

Asking right and powerful questions is considered as an important skill, simply because the right question provokes our thought process and subsequently triggers an action. The leader is expected to ask appropriate questions to clarify his understanding, dig deeper to elicit more information and to discover the truth in a given situation.

Questioning is an important tool.

A leader needs to keep a close tab on multiple, simultaneous events taking place all the time at work. In addition to standard reports, emails and status updates, the leader has a powerful tool to get the pulse of the project: asking right questions at the right time.

Think again before asking a question.

There is a time and place for all questions. A good leader should avoid a trap of thinking that he must keep asking questions. Listen well and then ask questions based on what you know.

Questioning is empowering.

When a leader asks a right, powerful question, not only it empowers the team member to rethink and find more options, but it also creates a sense of competence in the person. The good question also breaks current perceptions and behavior patterns, allowing a person to open up his mind and see beyond conventional horizons.

A sk questions, do not interrogate.

There is a thin line between questioning and interrogating. To question is to inquire, ask for information or pose something for consideration or reflection. To interrogate is to do the same but with greater intensity, more thoroughness and generally with authority. Questioning is for discovery but interrogating is grilling and carries negative connotation.

By a simple change in volume and tone of a question, accompanying facial expressions and gestures, questioning turns into interrogation inadvertently. Interrogating a team member puts him off or makes him defensive and it must be avoided.

Do not just ask questions, understand them too.

The new leader needs to develop an ability to analyze and understand the questions asked by the team members. These questions provide valuable information about what is going on in the person's mind.

What you do not ask can haunt you.

As the questions asked by the leader can shape his success, the questions he *fails* to ask can contribute to his failure. The new leader must develop courage and confidence so that he does not fail in asking right questions at the right time.

Acknowledging: The skill with the highest ROI.

Acknowledging is an act of expressing full appreciation for what the person is and for what he/she has done.

For a new leader, acknowledging has the highest ROI (Return on Investment) value in his pursuit to build trust. Acknowledging is very easy to practice, has almost always no-cost or low-cost, yet so powerful that it works wonders for a new manager.

Don't wait to acknowledge.

The promotions, bonuses and rewards are part of the corporate life but they happen only once or twice a year. Between these formal events of appreciation, informal, right-on-time, public and/or private occurrences of acknowledgement go a long way. It ensures that the team members feel accepted, included, and important.

Acknowledge by offering more authority and responsibility.

There are so many ways in which you can acknowledge your team members. You can be as creative as you want.

Grant a team member an authority as well as responsibility of a particular task or area of work. Handling the assignment independently and successfully will not only make him proud of himself but you will start developing a future leader in your team.

Acknowledgement could be done without spending.

It is important to note that acknowledging could be done without spending anything. Some of the easy and helpful ways of acknowledging your team members are:

- Public recognition of a milestone achieved, a task well done
- A special mention to a higher manager about someone's achievement / performance
- Personal voice message, email or handwritten note to the team member
- Assigning a highly desired, visible role
- Allowing extra time off, recommendation for a training class or inviting a family-member for a team event

Create your own acknowledgement fund.

As a leader of a team, you will have many opportunities to acknowledge your team members with something special when someone performs extra-ordinarily.

You can simply create your own fund for such special occasions. Start keeping away $25 a month for your own acknowledgement fund. When you want to recognize an out of the ordinary performance, you can use this fund. What can you use this fund for? Here are some ideas:

- Movie tickets for a couple
- Business/fiction best-seller book
- Subscription for a hobby/technical magazine
- Gift card from Amazon.com

Leader *is also an advisor.*

The team members look up to their leader for his counsel, recommendations and suggestions. In short, they treat you as their advisor in the work context. For a leader this is a great opportunity to share his knowledge, expertise and experience with the team and establishing himself.

Share your personal experiences.

When a leader is advising, he can share appropriate personal experiences with the team members. When a personal experience is shared as an advice, there is a human element added to information, making it more authentic and credible.

Of course, the leader must ensure that it is legally appropriate to share a particular personal experience in the professional situation. In any case, the team member is free to accept, reject or partially accept the advice and makes his/her own decision on how to use it.

Challenge your team.

Challenges are vital for learning and growth. It is a supportive push that entices a person to explore, question or revalidate the established facts or conventional wisdom.

In the work context, a leader can throw a challenge in a variety of ways: to design a new process, to complete a complex task within a strict deadline or to handle a tricky customer situation with a win-win approach. Good leaders are never satisfied and keep raising the bar constantly. Raising the bar and rewarding the behaviors that achieve higher goals is the best way to motivate team members to reach new heights of performance.

Don't get trapped into something you can't sustain.

Some new leaders want to impress the team and start many new initiatives early on. For example: a monthly lunch meeting with the team.

It is great if you can sustain it on an ongoing basis. When it becomes a recurring expense to continue the activity, the management may ask you to curtail it. Instead of getting into such awkward situation, think before you start. Make sure you have all the resources for a substantial amount of time to support your new initiative.

Give constructive feedback.

A leader is expected to give feedback to his team on their performance problems and other workplace concerns. Generally, your team members want to know how to improve themselves and their work. Your constructive feedback will help them.

There is a subtle difference between feedback and criticism. Constructive feedback is given with a positive attitude and with good intentions to correct future problems. Criticism comes with a negative tone, is usually personal and is not solution-oriented.

Giving feedback is a powerful tool available to a leader if he uses it wisely.

Over communicate. It never hurts.

A primary job of a leader is to communicate. Keep communicating with your team as much as you can with all possible ways. The team members always want to understand what is going on in the workplace and what their leader wants to say about it.

Be aware of your new role while inter-acting with your manager.

As a team leader, your interaction with your manager changes subtly. Now, you report to him in two capacities: as a team leader of your team and as a team player in his team. These two roles are overlapping and demand different skills. Be mindful of your dual role. Transitioning between the two roles will come to you by practice.

Learn *how to interact with the higher management.*

Anyone above your own manager is higher management for you. These positions are generally senior managers, directors and vice presidents. In your previous role as a team player, you might not have an opportunity to interact with this layer of management. As a new team leader, there will be many occasions when you will deal with the higher management.

You will need to pay attention to how you present yourself. It takes time, needs political savvy and continuous learning to be successful with the higher ups. As a new leader, request your own manager to mentor you in this area.

Your peer managers are your resources.

When you become a new manager, you enter into a layer of management where some more people are already occupying the places. These peer-level managers will have different levels of experiences and expertise areas. You have a lot to learn from each of them – especially about interacting with your common boss. Developing and maintaining cordial relationship with your peers is a simple strategy to start with.

Don't *miss the opportunity to develop yourself.*

Becoming a team leader presents you an unprecedented opportunity to develop yourself in many areas.

It is a common knowledge that the team leader has a responsibility to develop his team and help the team members to grow. At the same time, you need to pay close attention to develop yourself in this new role.

To develop yourself you need to know more about yourself. You can learn use self-assessments tests to find out your own managerial style. Based on this learning, you can identify your strengths and weaknesses. You might hire a coach who will help you to capitalize on your strengths and become a better leader.

Make your meetings meaningful.

As a new manager, you have an opportunity to get rid of those boring, unproductive, run-of-the-mill meetings. Be bold to redefine the structure and rules of your meetings so that people *want* to attend them.

Here are some aspects of creating an effective meeting:

- Clearly mark who must attend and who has an option to attend the meeting.
- Keep the meetings as short as possible. For a weekly team meeting, one hour is generally enough.
- Have an agenda for each meeting and allocate time to each speaker/presenter.
- Entrust someone to take minutes and action-items in the meeting. Make this person responsible for sending a list of action-items with respective owners and with the due dates, within 24 hours.

Continuous improvement is a key idea.

A leader is successful when he develops himself and his team members. You need to embrace an idea of continuous improvement to achieve development.

You can integrate this idea in your routine in many ways. Some of them are:

- Attending training classes once a quarter
- Reading a new book a month pertaining to your work area
- Declare Friday afternoon as exploration time when you and your team members are allowed to work on whatever they want and learn from the experience.

Don't hide the bad news.

As a leader, you may face situations when you need to share a bad news with your team. Don't hide the bad news, it always leaks and hurts you later.

News about company lay-off, reduction in budget and bonus, someone's poor performance are some of the examples which you are supposed to convey to your team members. Many managers think that their team members won't be able to take it. On the contrary, when handled with careful wording and poise, most people accept it gracefully.

Team building needs your efforts.

As a leader of the group, you need to take extra efforts to build true team spirit.

Managers can use traditional team building activities like group lunches and having a weekend picnic in the park. Some other ways are:

- Volunteering as a group for a common social cause.
- Developing a group website and sharing personal stories and pictures.
- Having a monthly meeting to share new learning, experiences and ideas or to listen to a guest speaker.

Accept that politics is natural in any workplace.

In any structured organization, politics is always present. As a new leader, you must understand the dynamics of politics instead of being naïve about it or ignoring it.

Don't try to eradicate politics altogether. Your best bet is to keep it as minimum as possible with some simple ideas:

- Create a challenging work environment with large goals to achieve. When people focus on achieving the results, there is no time for politics.
- Be upfront and communicate often with the team. When you have built trust with your team, the power of politics diminishes.
- Build visual displays of goals, actions and problems so that the facts are public and there is no chance for gossiping.

About the Author

Mandar Kulkarni is a senior project management consultant, business and life coach, speaker, entrepreneur, IT professional and his own words, 'a curious creature'.

After spending almost two decades playing various roles in the field of IT consulting, Mandar has founded Millennium Mantra, Inc., a professional consulting and coaching company, serving the corporate and individual clients. In addition to his MBA and PMP qualifications, he is a graduate of the Coach University, a premier coach training school in the world. Mandar has a passion to apply the coaching principles to the disciplines he is already familiar with: management and project management. Along with his consulting practice, Mandar runs his own teleclass-based program at PMPCoaching.com where he conducts coaching programs to help prepare for project management certification exams. He is an active volunteer at PMI's Silicon Valley chapter as a Director of Certifications. He also volunteers as an IT Director for California Arts Association.

Mandar lives in Fremont, California. You can reach him by email at Mandar@MillenniumMantra.com.

Contact Us

We, at Millennium Mantra, Inc provide following services to the business and individual clients.

- Project Management Consulting
- Workshops, seminars and speeches on using Personal Coaching principles in
    - corporate and professional environment
    - school environment
- Group Coaching for project teams at work
- Individual Coaching in Life, Career and Parenting

Contact us to learn more how we can help you:

- Web: www.MillenniumMantra.com
- Call: 510-402-4561
- Email: Sales@MillenniumMantra.com